CAPE POETRY

ROGER McGOUGH
HOLIDAY ON DEATH ROW

by the same author

SUMMER WITH MONIKA
WATCHWORDS
AFTER THE MERRYMAKING
OUT OF SEQUENCE
GIG
SPORTING RELATIONS
IN THE GLASSROOM
WAVING AT TRAINS

Roger McGough

HOLIDAY ON DEATH ROW

JONATHAN CAPE
THIRTY-TWO BEDFORD SQUARE LONDON

First published 1979
Reprinted 1981, 1983, 1988
© 1979 by Roger McGough

Jonathan Cape Ltd
32 Bedford Square, London WC1B 3SG

British Library Cataloguing in Publication Data

McGough, Roger
Holiday on Death Row.
I. Title
821'.9'14   PR6063.A219H/

ISBN 0-224-01693-8

Printed in Great Britain by
St Edmundsbury Press, Bury St Edmunds, Suffolk
Bound by Richard Clay (The Chaucer Press) Ltd
Bungay, Suffolk

Contents

An apology 7

Just another Autumn day 8

Vegetarians 9

The lake 10

May Ball 12

Contact lenses 13

Incident at a Presidential Garden Party 14

Tide and time 15

W.P.C. Marjorie Cox 16

Mouth 17

Passion 19

Funny sort of bloke 20

Vague impressions 21

Closet fascist 23

Nocturne 24

10 Ways to Make a Killing on the Stock Market 25

Solarium 26

A golden life 27

The horse's mouth 29

The Rot 31

War of the Roses 32

Cabbage 33

Missed 35

'Take a poem, Miss Smith.' 36

His poems are nets 37

The death of John Berryman in slow motion 39

Blazing fruit 40

Poem for a dead poet 41

Survivor 42

Holiday on Death Row 43

An apology

Owing to an increase
in the cost of printing
this poem will be less
than the normal length.

In the face of continued
economic crises, strikes,
unemployment and V.A.T.
it offers no solutions.

Moreover, because of
a recent work-to-rule
imposed by the poet
it doesn't even rhyme.

Just another Autumn day

In Parliament, the Minister
for Mists and Mellow Fruitfulness
announces, that owing to
inflation and rising costs
there will be no Autumn
next year. September, October
and November are to be
cancelled, and the Government
to bring in the 'Callaghannual'
or nine-month year instead.
Thus will we all live longer.

Emergency measures are to be
introduced to combat outbreaks
of well-being, and feelings
of elation inspired by the season.
Breathtaking sunsets will be
restricted to alternate Fridays
and gentle dusks prohibited.
Fallen leaves will be outlawed
and persons found in possession
of conkers, imprisoned without trial.
Thus will we all work harder.

The announcement caused little reaction.
People either way don't really care
No time have they to stand and stare
Looking for work or slaving away
Just another Autumn day.

Vegetarians

Vegetarians are cruel, unthinking people.
Everybody knows that a carrot screams when grated.
That a peach bleeds when torn apart.
Do you believe an orange insensitive
to thumbs gouging out its flesh?
That tomatoes spill their brains painlessly?
Potatoes, skinned alive and boiled,
the soil's little lobsters.
Don't tell me it doesn't hurt
when peas are ripped from the scrotum,
the hide flayed off sprouts,
cabbage shredded, onions beheaded.

Throw in the trowel
and lay down the hoe.
Mow no more
Let my people go!

The lake

For years there have been no fish in the lake.
People hurrying through the park avoid it like the plague.
Birds steer clear and the sedge of course has withered.
Trees lean away from it, and at night it reflects,
not the moon, but the blackness of its own depths.
There are no fish in the lake. But there is life there.
There is life ...

Underwater pigs glide between reefs of coral debris.
They love it here. They breed and multiply
in sties hollowed out of the mud
and lined with mattresses and bedsprings.
They live on dead fish and rotting things,
drowned pets, plastic and assorted excreta.
Rusty cans they like the best.
Holding them in webbed trotters
their teeth tear easily through the tin
and poking in a snout
they noisily suck out
the putrid matter within.

There are no fish in the lake. But there is life there.
There is life ...

For on certain evenings after dark
shoals of pigs surface and look out
at those houses near the park.
Where, in bathrooms, children feed stale bread to plastic ducks
and in attics, toyyachts have long since runaground.
Where, in livingrooms, anglers dangle their lines
on patterned carpets, and bemoan the fate
of the ones that got away.

Down on the lake, piggy eyes glisten.
They have acquired a taste for flesh.
They are licking their lips. Listen ...

May Ball

The evening lay before us
like her silken dress
arranged carefully over the bed.
It would be a night to remember.
We would speak of it often
in years to come. There would
be good food and wine,
cabaret, and music to dance to.
How we'd dance.
How we'd laugh.
We would kiss indiscreetly,
and what are lawns for
but to run barefoot across?

But the evening didn't do
what it was told.
It's the morning after now
and morningafter cold.
I don't know what went wrong
but I blame her. After all
I bought the tickets.
Of course, I make no mention,
that's not my style,
and I'll continue to write
at least for a while.
I carry her suitcase down to the hall,
our first (and her last) University Ball.

Contact lenses

Somenights
she leaves them in
until after they have made love.
She likes to see clearly
the lines and curves of bodies.
To watch his eyes, his mouth.
Somenights she enjoys that.

Othernights
when taken by the mood
she takes them out before
and abandons herself
to her blurred stranger.
Other senses compete to compensate.
All is flesh. Looks bigger too.

Incident at a Presidential Garden Party

Taking tea on the lawn. Uninvited,
a lorry skids through the flower beds.
Tables are turned, salads tossed
to the grass, canapés to the wind.

Creamcakes and colonels squelch
in the mad career.
Waiters scream, tyres squeal,
underlings crunched underwheel.

Out of control, the lorry
surges towards The President.
No one moves. Screech, smash,
smithereens.   Then silence.

The Great Man dusts his suit,
ensures his tie is straight.
The lorry is given the Kiss of Life.
But too late.

Tide and time

My Aunty Jean
was no mean hortihorologist.
For my fifteenth birthday
she gave me a floral wristwatch.
Wormproof and self-weeding,
its tick was as soft
as a butterfly on tiptoe.

All summer long
I sniffed happily the passing hours.
Until late September
when, forgetting to take it off
before bathing at New Brighton,
the tide washed time away.

W.P.C. Marjorie Cox

W.P.C. Marjorie Cox
brave as a lion
bright as an ox
is above all else, a girl.
Large of bosom
soft of curl.

Keeps in her dainty vanity case
diamanté handcuffs, trimmed with lace,
a golden whistle, a silken hanky,
a photograph of Reg Bosanquet
(signed: 'To Marjorie, with love'),
a truncheon in a velvet glove.

W.P.C. Marjorie Cox
cute as a panda
in bobby sox.
Men queue to loiter with intent
for the pleasure of an hour spent
in her sweet custody.

Mouth

I went to the mirror
but the mirror was bare,
looked for my mouth
but my mouth wasn't there.
Over the lips had grown
a whiskered hymen of skin.

I went to the window
wanting to shout
I pictured the words
but nothing came out.
The face beneath the nose
an empty hoarding.

And as I waited, I could feel
flesh filling in the space behind.
Teeth melted away tasting of snow
as the stalactites of the palate
joined the stalagmites below.
The tongue, like a salted snail,
sweated and shrivelled.

The doctor has suggested plastic surgery:
a neat incision, cosmetic dentistry
and full red lips (factory fresh).
He meant well but I declined.

After all, there are advantages.
At last I have given up smoking,
and though food is a needle
twice a day, it needs no cooking.
There is little that I miss.
I never could whistle and there's no one to kiss.

In the street, people pass by
unconcerned. I give no one directions
and in return am given none.
When asked if I am happy
I look the inquisitor straight in the eye
and think to myself ... ("

")

Passion

We keep our noses clean, my friend and i,
do what we're told.
Keep profiles soft and low
as we grow old.

We take up little space, my friend and i,
avoid the town.
Keep our curtains drawn
our voices down.

We live an ordered life, my friend and i,
cause little fuss.
If only everyone
could be like us.

       *   *   *   *

Screaming now, he screams, my friend, and i
know what to do.
Have him put away.
(Well wouldn't you?)

Funny sort of bloke

Have you heard the latest scandal
About 80-year-old Mr Brown?
He stole from Matron's handbag
Then hitchhiked into town.

Had a slap-up meal at the Wimpy
Then went to a film matinée
One of them sexy blue ones
We're not supposed to see.

Then he bought some jeans and a toupee
Spent the night in a pub
Then carried on till the early hours
Dancing in a club.

They caught him in the morning
Trying to board the London train
He tried to fight them off
But he's back here once again.

They asked him if he'd be a good boy
He said he'd rather not
So they gave him a nice injection
And tied him up in his cot.

He died that very night
Apparently a stroke.
Kept screaming: 'Come out Death and fight.'
Funny sort of bloke.

Vague impressions

Ossie Edwards couldn't punch a hole in a wet echo.
He was no fighter.
And if he wasn't thicker than 2 short planks
he wasn't much brighter.
To compensate, he did impressions.
Impressions of trains, impressions of planes,
of James Cagney, Humphrey Bogart and Roy Rogers.
They all sounded the same.
On the 3rd year Cosa Nostra
his impressions made little impression
so he became bully fodder.

Then, quite suddenly, Ossie saw the light.
One Monday morning during R.I.
he switched to birdcalls.
Peewits, kestrels, tomtits and kingfishers
he became them all.
Larks and nightingales.
The birdnotes burst from his throat
like a host of golden buckshot.
And as the nearest any of us got to ornithology
was playing football on a debris with a dead pigeon
there could be no argument.
So he was rechristened 'Percy'
and left alone.
And left alone
he twittered his way happily to 3 'O' levels
and a job in a shipping office.

'Twas there he met Sylvia
whom he courted and married.
She took an interest in his hobby
and they were soon appearing in local concerts:
'The Sylvatones — Bird Impressionists'.
The double-act ended however
when Sylvia left him for a widower
who taught her how to sing.
Her love for Perce she realised
never was the real thing,
but, like his impressions, a tuneful imitation.

And that was years ago and still
whenever I pass that way at night
and hear the shrill
yearning hoot of an owl,
I imagine Percy
perched out there in the darkness,
lonely, obsessed.
Calling for his love
to return to the nest.

Closet fascist

in the staffroom
or over drinks
he says the things
with which he thinks
his colleagues will concur:
anti-Powell, anti-Front
liberalminded, fair.

But enthroned alone
in his W.C.
on toilet paper
signs a decree
deporting immigrants en masse.
Salutes the mob
then wipes his ass.

Nocturne

Unable to sleep.
Every sound an enemy.
each stirring an intruder.

Even my own breathing
is frisked
before being allowed out.

I suffer during darkness
a thousand bludgeonings,
see blood everywhere.

How my poor heart
dreads the night
shift. I wear

a smear of sweat
like a moist plastercast.
Adrift in a monstered sea.

Those actors who scare so well
in your nightmares
have all practised first on me.

10 Ways to Make a Killing on the Stock Market

1   Get out of bed early and frequently.
    Remember, punctuality is the investor's best friend.

2   Resist the temptation to dress too gaudily.

3   Keep your figures neat and your columns orderly.

4   Avoid fatty foods.

5   Whatever you do ... Whichever way we ... I mean.

6   Your face. I think of your face. Your body.

7   Enfranchise non-voting 'A' shares through a rights issue.

8   Pain. The tears. But the laughter. We must never forget the laughter.

9   Not too late. Don't leave me. Please don't leave ...

10

Solarium

i own a solarium
and when it's cold
i simmer in
artificial gold

i keep away
from mornings grey
my private sun
smiles down all day

i pity those
whose flesh is white
as bronzed i sleep
alone each night

A golden life

We live a simple life
my wife and I. Are
the envy of our friends.
We are artists. Skilled craftsmen.
I am good with my hands
She with hers.
I am a goldsmith
She a masseuse.

I design and make
gold lockets that cannot be opened
necklaces that will not fasten
ornate keys for which there are no locks.
Trinkets to buy and hoard
toys for the rich and bored.
Things useless, but beautiful.

Compared with the objects I make,
I am dull.
My wife is not dull,
She is exciting.
After a hard day at the parlor
or visiting hotels
(I do not pry)
She comes home
tired, but exciting.

I give her something golden
each evening something new.
It makes her smile.

She rewards me with her golden body
which I melt and shape at will.
Fashioning, with consummate skill,
the precious metal of her flesh.

We live a golden life
my wife and I. Dream
golden dreams. And
each golden morning
go our golden ways.
Make golden dreams for strangers.
Golden nights
and golden days.

The horse's mouth

They bought the horse
in Portobello
brought it home
could hardly wait
installed it in the living room
next to knitted dinner plate

Next to ashtray
(formerly bedpan)
euphonium
no one can play
camel-saddle dollypeg
wooden gollywog with tray

Near a neo
deco lampshade
(a snip at
thirty-seven quid)
castanets and hula-hoop
trunk with psychedelic lid

Under front end
of a caribou
next to foam-
filled rollerskate
(made by a girl in Camden Lock
—she of knitted dinner plate)

Uprooted from
its carousel
the painted horse

now laid to waste
amidst expensive bric-à-brac
and sterile secondhand bad taste

      *   *   *   *

And each night as Mr and Ms Trend
in brassbed they lie dreaming
the horse in downstairs darkness
mouths a silent screaming.

The Rot

Some years ago the Rot set in.
It began in a corner of the bedroom
following the birth of the second child.
It spread into the linen cupboard
and across the fabric of our lives.
Experts came to treat it.
Could not.
The Rot could not be stopped.

Dying now, we live with it.
The fungus grows.
It spreads across our faces.
We watch the smiles rot,
gestures crumble.
Diseased, we become the disease.
Part of the fungus.
The part that dreams. That feels pain.

We are condemned.
Things dying, that flaunt their dying,
that cannot hide, are demolished.
We will rot eachother no longer.
From the street outside
comes the sound of the drill,
as men, hungry for dust,
close in for the kill.

War of the Roses

Friday came the news.
Her G.P. rang and told her.
The telephone buckled
in her hand. Safely distanced,
he offered to come round.
'Why bother,' she said, 'Bastard.'

She had guessed anyway. The body
had been telling her for months.
Sending haemorrhages, eerie messages
of bruises. Outward signs
of inner turmoil. You can't sweep
blood under the carpet.

Thirty, single, living with and for
a four-year-old daughter. Smokes,
drinks whisky, works in television.
Wakes around four each morning
fearful and crying. Listens to
the rioting in her veins.

Her blood is at war with itself.
With each campaign more pain,
a War of the Roses over again.
She is a battlefield. In her,
Red and White armies compete.
She is a pair of crossed swords
on the medical map of her street.

Cabbage

(after 'I like that stuff' by Adrian Mitchell)

Humphrey Bogart died of it
People are terrified of it
             cancer
      I hate that stuff

Groucho was laid low with it
One in five of us will go with it
             heart attack
      I hate that stuff

Monroe's life turned sour on it
Hancock spent his last half hour on it
             sleeping pills
      I hate that stuff

Hendrix couldn't wait for it
Chemistshops stay open late for it
             heroin
      I hate that stuff

Mama Cass choked on it
Blankets get soaked in it
             vomit
      I hate that stuff

Women learn to live with it
No one can live without it
             blood
      I hate that stuff

Hospitals are packed with it
Saw my mother racked with it
            pain
        I hate that stuff

Few like to face the truth of it
We're all living proof of it
            death
        I hate that stuff

Schoolboys are forcefed with it
Cattle are served dead with it
            cabbage
        I hate that stuff

Missed

out of work
divorced
usually pissed.

he aimed
low in life
and
        missed.

'Take a poem, Miss Smith.'

'Take a poem, Miss Smith.
I will call it *The Ploughman*.
"The ploughman wearily follows the plough,
The dust that lies upon his brow,
Gnarled as the dead oak tree bough,
Makes me think of how ... of how ... "
How nice you smell, Miss Smith.
Is it Chanel? I thought so.
But to work: "The ploughman wearily follows ... "
Ah, but I am wearied of ploughing.
File it away under "Nature – unfinished".

'Take a poem, Miss Smith.
It is entitled *Ulster '79*
"Along the Shankhill Road, a pall
Of smoke hangs, thick as ... thick as ... "
Hair, something different about the hair.
A new style? It suits you.
But where was I? Oh yes:
"Along the Shankhill Road ... "
No, I feel unpolitical today.
Put it away in the file
marked "Wars – unfinished".

'Take a poem, Miss Smith.
It will be known as *Flesh*.
"The flesh I love to touch
Is soft as ... soft as ... "
Take off your blouse, Miss Smith,
I feel a love poem coming on ... '

His poems are nets

His poems are nets
in which he hopes
to capture girls

He makes them at work
or late at night
when pubs are closed

He uses materials
at hand. Scraps
of conversation, jokes,

lines lifted from
dead poets (he likes
a bit of poetry in his poems)

*   *   *   *

He washes his hair
for the reading
and wears tight pants

When it comes to him
he swaggers out
unzipping his file

Exposes small dreams
which he breaks
with a big stick

His verse a mag
nifying glass
held up to his prick

*   *   *   *

His poems are nets
and like nets
can be seen through

Girls bide their time
Wait for the singer
to throw them a line.

The death of John Berryman in slow motion

We open on a frozen river
(the spot where the poet has arranged to meet death).
The whiteness is blinding.
The glare hurts our eyes.

From somewhere above he jumps.
We see the shadow first
seeping into the ice
like a bruise. Thickening.

There is no sound but the wind
skulking beneath the bridge.

Now the body comes into shot.
Falling, blurred, a ragged bearskin.
The shadow opens its arms to greet it.

The wind is holding its breath.

We freeze frame at the moment of impact
(noting the look of surprise on the poet's face).
We then pan slowly upwards
to the grey Minnesota sky.

Fade to black.

Blazing fruit

(or The Role of the Poet as Entertainer)

During dinner the table caught fire.
No one alluded to the fact
and we ate on, regardless of
the flames singeing our conversation.

Unaware of the smoke
and the butlers swooning,
topics ranged from Auden
to Zefferelli. I was losing
concentration however, and being
short on etiquette, became tense
and began to fidget with the melting cutlery.

I was fashioning a spoon
into a question mark
when the Chablis began to steam
and bubble. I stood up,
mumbled something about having left the gas running
and fled blushing
across the plush terrain of the carpet.

The tut-tut-tutting could be heard above
the cra-cra-cracking of the bone china.

Outside, I caught a cab
to the nearest bus stop.
While, back at the table,
they were toying with blazing fruit
and discussing the Role of the Poet as Entertainer,
when the roof fell in.

Poem for a dead poet

He was a poet he was.
A proper poet.
He said things
that made you think
and said them nicely.
He saw things
that you or I
could never see
and saw them clearly.
He had a way
with language.
Images flocked around
him like birds,
St Francis, he was,
of the words. Words?
Why he could almost make 'em talk.

Survivor

Everyday
I think about dying.
About disease, starvation,
violence, terrorism, war,
the end of the world.

It helps
keep my mind off things.

Holiday on Death Row

new dead flowers in
living room. First
Wasp of Spring. Time
for writing. Sap and
dying. Ashes and seed
lie scattered etc.
In kitchen, Wife
cook sunday dinner
for herself. Upstairs
Husband push drawing
pins into scowling
mouth of penis.

2

Wife is out. Has taken
clichés to launderette.
Husband, withdrawn, stare
overlong at photographs
of himself, in hope
of being recognised.
In front of mirrors
he bob and weave,
turn suddenly to catch
reflection off guard.
Reflection always on time.
On occasions, lying in wait.

3

Wife, downstairs midnight
putting cholesterol in his
Flora, decide their life
together has become anathema.
Stuffed toad in birdcage.
Husband, upstairs writing
poems she will never
read, decide holiday
abroad would be best
thing for both of them.
Next day he leave for Anathema.
Wife give toad kiss of life.

4

Husband,   penis   loaded
with   drawing   pins,   swagger
into   kitchen.   Unimpressed,
Wife   snarl   matteroffactly.
'You   rat   a   tat   tat
      rat   a   tat   tat
Take   that   a   tat   tat.'
Wife   is   pinned   against   wall
like   fading   Wanted   Poster.
Husband   pack   away
empty   shotgun   and   return
upstairs   to   collect   reward.

5

she hang on his every word.
Pull, pull and pull.
Hands to his mouth
he fight back. Wife
drag him to floor.
Words cry out in pain:
'Words, we're only words,
we don't mean anything.'
Wife release grip
and return to kitchen.
'That what you always
say.' She say.

in Husband's dreams, her
stockings burst at seams.
She is centre-fold
of all his magazines.
Pinned up each night,
she disport herself
as he befit. As he
thought she used to do
or might have done.
Prickteasing series of
saucy pix. His memory
playing safe, playing tricks.

except for sound of their breathing.
In bed Husband mustn't touch.
Put arms around body he
helped shape. He fight impulse.
Do what is not natural.
Keep his self to himself.
Nerve ends tingle. He become
Electric Chair and move in.
She asleep on Death Row.
He wonder what would be
her last request. Chair
get erection. Chair know best.

8

Wife hoard hazelnuts
in cunt. Husband
train squirrels to
fetch hazelnuts. Wife
keep fox in petticoats
to chase squirrels. At
break of day, Husband,
in coat so gay, unleash
hounds in bedroom to catch
fox. Wife join Anti-blood-
sports League. Husband join
Anti-nuts-in-cunts Brigade.

Wife want life of own.

Husband want life of Wife.

Husband hire hitman.

Hitman hit Wife.

Wife hit back.

Hit, hitman run.

Wife run harder.

Hurt hitman.

Hurt hitman hit Husband.

Tired Husband hire second
hitman to fire first hitman.

Fired hitman retire, hurt.

Husband keep live rat down
front of jeans for rainy day.
One rainy day, drunk on
cooking sherry, Wife slip
hand inside Husband's jeans.
With brutal strokes she
skin it alive before
pulling off its head.
Wiping blood on pinny
she return to cakemix.
Husband bury dead rat
for another year.

upstairs, Husband wrestle
with major themes. Wife
in kitchen putting
two and two together.
Always Wife in kitchen.
Always Husband wrestling.
On kitchen table is
flour, water, drawing pins,
salt, blood, ashes etc.
On desk upstairs,
major themes (or parts
thereof) lie scattered etc.

photographs of hitmen.
Hazelnuts for rainy day.
Dead flowers in fading
penis. Clichéd toad
bursting at seams. Empty
shotgun in birdcage. Holiday
on Death Row. Words,
we're only words.
Husband, upstairs, painting
out light in painting
of end of tunnel. Wife
in garden, digging up rat.